21st Century Skills Library

REAL WORLD MATH: SPORTS

TENNIS

Katie Marsico and Cecilia Minden

Cherry Lake Publishing
Ann Arbor, Michigan

Published in the United States of America by Cherry Lake Publishing
Ann Arbor, Michigan
www.cherrylakepublishing.com

Math Adviser: Tonya Walker, MA, Boston University

Content Adviser: Thomas Sawyer, EdD, Professor of Recreation and Sport Management,
Indiana State University

Photo Credits: Cover and page 1, ©iStockphoto.com/McIninch; pages 4 and 9, ©Galina
Barskaya, used under license from Shutterstock, Inc.; page 7, ©iStockphoto.com/
Jiblet; page 10, ©iStockphoto.com/cscredon; page 12, ©iStockphoto.com/xjben; page
14, ©Lance Bellers, used under license from Shutterstock, Inc.; page 17, 18, and 21,
©Associated Sports Photography/Alamy; page 23, ©AP Photo/Jytte Nielsen; page 25,
©iStockphoto.com/barsik; page 27, ©iStockphoto.com/epicurean

Library of Congress Cataloging-in-Publication Data
Marsico, Katie, 1980–
Tennis / by Katie Marsico and Cecilia Minden.
   p. cm.—(Real world math)
Includes bibliographical references and index.
ISBN-13: 978-1-60279-248-7
ISBN-10: 1-60279-248-8
1. Tennis—Juvenile literature. 2. Arithmetic—Problems, exercises,
etc.—Juvenile literature. I. Minden, Cecilia. II. Title. III. Series.
GV996.5.M37 2009
796.342—dc22   2008001179

*Cherry Lake Publishing would like to acknowledge the work of
The Partnership for 21st Century Skills.
Please visit* www.21stcenturyskills.org *for more information.*

TABLE OF CONTENTS

CHAPTER ONE

WHAT A SERVE!

Returning a serve can be as hard as serving the ball. You need to be prepared, watch the ball, and use some math skills to succeed.

You take a deep breath and study your opponent on the other side of the tennis court. It is important to try to guess how she will hit the ball. Smack! The ball bounces off of her racket and onto your part of the court. Will you be quick enough to get the ball back over the net?

You dive forward and slap the ball upward with your racket. It flies over the net. Your opponent is not fast enough, though. She misses the ball, and you have just won the game! This game helped you win your third set and the entire match. Would you believe that your math skills also helped you to become a champion on the tennis court?

REAL WORLD MATH CHALLENGE

C. J. is playing tennis with Jake. Both players know that someone has to score at least 4 points to win a game. They have played 5 games so far. The winner of each game has scored exactly 4 points. C. J. has won 2 games. **How many games has Jake won? How many points has C. J. scored so far? How many points has Jake scored?**

(Turn to page 29 for the answers)

How important is math to tennis? First, you need to know a little bit about the sport. Tennis is a game in which players use rackets to hit a ball over a net. A game of singles involves two players. A game of doubles includes two teams of two players each. Tennis can be played on an indoor or outdoor court.

Tennis has been around for hundreds of years. Players used to hit a ball back and forth with the palms of their hands. Eventually, people began using paddles and rackets.

A man named Walter C. Wingfield created tennis kits in 1873. His kits included a set of rules and different pieces of equipment. Men and women used the kits for tennis games at outdoor parties. Soon, his game took hold around the world.

The U.S. National Lawn Tennis Association was formed in 1881. It soon changed its name to the U.S. Tennis Association (USTA). Founders started arranging competitions called tournaments. The

Tennis has fans around the world. This match takes place on a grass court at Wimbledon in England.

USTA is now the largest tennis organization in the world. It has more than 700,000 members. It oversees **professional** tennis in the United States.

Four important yearly tournaments are the Australian Open, the French Open, Wimbledon, and the U.S. Open. This group of games is known as the Grand Slam. A player who wants to win the Grand Slam must claim all four **titles** in a single **calendar year**! Winning the Grand Slam is not easy, but some talented athletes such as Venus Williams and Serena Williams have done it.

Tennis also includes international team competitions. The Davis Cup is the international team competition for men. The Fed Cup is the international team competition for women.

Now you have a little background information on tennis. It is time to learn the rules of the game. You are also ready to find out how math comes into play on the court. Grab your racket and your calculator. Get set to serve like a winner!

CHAPTER TWO

A FEW TENNIS BASICS

A woman serves in a doubles match. Doubles players use the outside lines as boundaries.

Many people don't realize that tennis involves measurements and math.

Tennis is played on a precisely measured court that is in the shape of a

rectangle. People playing doubles usually use a court that is 78 feet (23.8

meters) long and 36 feet (11.0 m) wide. People playing singles are often on

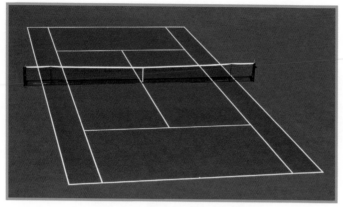

No matter what surface you play on, you must know the meaning of each white line on the court.

a court that is 78 feet (23.8 m) long but only 27 feet (8.2 m) wide. Tennis courts can be made from different materials, such as asphalt, clay, concrete, grass, and wood. There are white lines painted on the court. Each line has a different meaning.

Boundary lines at the ends of the court are called baselines. A short line called a hash mark falls in the middle of each baseline. Service lines are parallel to the baselines but are closer to the middle of the court. Whoever is serving the ball must hit it into the area between his opponent's service line and the net. A center service line divides the two service lines. The center service line creates areas called service boxes, or service courts. The net runs across the width of the court and is parallel to the baselines. The top of the net is 3 feet (0.9 m) from the ground at the center of the court.

Doubles sidelines mark boundaries when doubles play. Singles sidelines stretch parallel to the doubles sidelines but are closer to the middle of the court. They are used when singles play.

The player who serves must hit the ball so that it travels diagonally into her opponent's service box. Why is it so important that tennis players pay attention to all these lines and measurements?

The point of the game is to score by hitting the ball so that the other player is unable to return it. Players return the ball by hitting it back over the net before it bounces twice. It must land on or inside the boundary lines of the other player's side of the court.

A powerful, well-placed serve is an important skill in tennis. Andy Roddick holds the record for the fastest recorded serve—155 miles (249 kilometers) per hour!

Whoever is serving the ball is known as the server. The player who returns the serve is called the receiver. Every game, the serve alternates between sides. A fault occurs when a player serves a ball that does not land in the service court. The server gets another chance, though. Sometimes the server misses the service court a second time. He then double-faults. The other player or team ends up gaining a point. A game of tennis that did not have lines or measurements would hardly be a game at all! It wouldn't take much skill for players to hit the ball wherever they wanted.

Athletes often begin a rally once the ball is served. This means they hit the ball back and forth several times until someone scores a point. Points can be scored in a few different ways. One way is to hit the ball so that the other player cannot return it. Another way is when an opponent hits the ball out-of-bounds or into the net.

Tennis players use special names to refer to scores. "Love" means a score of zero points. Whoever gets the first point has a score of 15.

Players use different **strokes** in tennis. Being a good tennis player means using one's judgment and reasoning to decide which stroke would be best. During a game, players must think quickly if they want to win.

One type of stroke is a ground stroke. This involves a player hitting the ball back over the net after it has bounced once. A volley occurs when a player hits the ball back before it bounces at all. Players who are close to the net can sometimes hit a drop shot. This means they softly and gently return the ball. A shot that is hit in a high arc is known as a lob. Players sometimes use a powerful overhead shot called a smash. Whatever the stroke, skilled tennis players are good at selecting the best method of sending the ball over the net.

Scoring in tennis adds another element of math. This match score is 3 games to 2 in the first set.

When players each have one point, the tied score is known as 15–all or 15–15. Whoever gains two points has a score of 30. A player who has three points is said to have a score of 40. A 40–40 tie is called a deuce.

Whichever player or team scores four points first wins the game. The exception is when both sides tie at three points each. These games must keep going until one

14

player or team gets two points ahead of the other side. The winner of the

first game is ahead in the first set 1–0. To win a set, a player must win at

least six games and be two games up on the opponent. The champions of a

match have to win the majority of sets. These players must win at least two

out of three sets or three out of five sets.

Tennis players wear clothes that help them stay cool and move quickly.

They often choose short skirts, shorts, and short-sleeved shirts. Some

women wear simple tennis dresses.

REAL WORLD MATH CHALLENGE

Bernard and Bella are playing each other in a tennis match. Bella wins 6 games
during the first set. Bernard wins 4. **What is the total number of games they
play during the first set? How many points does Bella win? How about
Bernard?** Remember that a player must score 4 points to win a game. Also keep
in mind that neither Bella nor Bernard ties at any point during the first set.

(Turn to page 29 for the answers)

Players wear special tennis shoes. Tennis shoes have flexible rubber bottoms. They help athletes move faster without sliding or slipping on the court.

There are no limits on how long a tennis match can last. Most matches take one to two hours. Players are allowed to take short breaks.

Perhaps you are wondering how you can keep all these details straight. Your math skills will help you understand the measurements and guidelines that are important to tennis!

CHAPTER THREE

DO THE MATH: IMPRESSIVE PROS

Who is your favorite tennis star? Players win fans with their outstanding skills on the court. German player Steffi Graf is one famous example. She retired in 1999 after a career filled with impressive statistics. She won all four Grand Slam tournaments

Steffi Graf of Germany was the Wimbledon ladies' champion in 1996. She won 22 Grand Slam singles titles during her career.

in women's singles in 1988. She also received an Olympic gold medal in tennis that same year. This amazing athlete was ranked the number-one

Venus and Serena Williams are sisters and amazing tennis pros. The Williams sisters grew up in Compton, a violent suburb of Los Angeles. As children, they were determined to improve their tennis skills and master the game. They practiced six hours a day, six days a week. They set high goals for themselves and achieved those goals. Venus has won an Olympic gold medal and 14 Grand Slam titles. Serena has claimed an Olympic gold medal and eight Grand Slam titles. Sometimes the sisters play together during tournaments. They have even competed against one another!

American champion Andre Agassi comes to the net to return a ball.

player in the world by the WTA for 377 weeks. Graf was welcomed into the International Tennis Hall of Fame in 2004.

Professional tennis has many record-setting male athletes, too. In fact,

Graf is married to one! American pro Andre Agassi is Graf's husband.

Agassi won in men's singles at Wimbledon in 1992 and at the U.S. Open

in 1994 and 1999. He claimed the same victory at the Australian Open in

1995, 2000, 2001, and 2003. He even won an Olympic gold medal in men's

singles in 1996. Agassi retired in 2006.

Tennis players are honored for their athletic talent in several ways.

Many receive trophies. Some are named Player of the Year or World

REAL WORLD MATH CHALLENGE

Steffi Graf played professional tennis from 1982 to 1999. She won 902 of the 1,017 singles matches she played during her career. Andre Agassi was a pro from 1986 to 2006. He played 1,144 singles matches and was the champion in 870 of them. **How many more singles matches did Graf win than her husband? What is the difference in the average number of matches they won each year during their careers?**

(Turn to page 29 for the answers)

Champion. Others are inducted into the International Tennis Hall of Fame.

Impressive numbers on the court can make a tennis star very popular.

These numbers can also affect the numbers on a player's paycheck.

Tennis pros can make a lot of money. Agassi earned $28.2 million in 2004.

You can see that tennis can lead to some incredible numbers!

REAL WORLD MATH CHALLENGE

Recall that Agassi earned $28.2 million in 2004. Assume that he made at least that much in 2005 and 2006. **What is the very least he would have earned during this 3-year period?**

(Turn to page 29 for the answer)

CHAPTER FOUR

DO THE MATH: REMARKABLE TENNIS RECORDS

Winning all four Grand Slam tournaments in a single calendar year is an amazing accomplishment. Would you believe that someone has actually done it twice? Australian pro Rod Laver was a champion in men's singles in both 1962 and 1969.

Rod Laver hits a backhand in 1971. Many people consider this Australian the greatest player in the history of tennis.

Some players win career grand slams. That means they don't win all

four tournaments in a calendar year. These athletes win each tournament

at least once, though. U.S. pro Serena Williams was only 21 when she

claimed a career grand slam in 2003.

REAL WORLD MATH CHALLENGE

A total of 5 singles players hold the record for winning all 4 Grand Slam
tournaments in a calendar year. Rod Laver is the only athlete to have won twice.
Three of the players are women. Two are men. Two of the players are from the
United States. **What percentage of the championships have been won by
men? What percentage of the championships have been won by women?
How many of the winning players are from countries other than the
United States?**

(Turn to page 29 for the answers)

Tennis is filled with incredible records. The United States holds the

record for the most Davis Cup victories. American players have won

*Sisters Venus (left) and Serena Williams celebrate
winning the ladies' doubles title at Wimbledon in 2000.
They have each won several Grand Slam titles.*

31 times. Don't forget the Fed Cup! American athletes have been the

champions a record 17 times.

You know that most matches last one to two hours. French players

Fabrice Santoro and Arnaud Clement set a record during the 2004 French

In 2007, Swiss pro Roger Federer broke the world record of being ranked number one the most weeks in a row by the ATP. The previous record was 160 weeks in a row at number one, held by tennis great Jimmy Connors. Earning the top rank is a huge accomplishment in the sports world. Officials who keep track of records must be able to carefully analyze and interpret numbers and information to determine a player's position. An athlete's career can depend on it!

Open. They battled each other on the court for 6 hours and 33 minutes.

Numbers are what shape tennis history. A record might be set the next time you watch a match. Maybe one day, you will even create records of your own.

REAL WORLD MATH CHALLENGE

The youngest player to win the U.S. Open was 15-year-old Vincent Richards in 1918. The oldest player to win was 49-year-old Martina Navratilova in 2006. **What is the average of their two ages? How many years passed between the tournaments?**

(Turn to page 29 for the answers)

CHAPTER FIVE

GET YOUR OWN GAME GOING!

*Success on the court starts with plenty of practice. Doubles
is a great way to practice with more than one friend.*

You do not have to be a professional athlete to enjoy tennis. Many

colleges, high schools, and grade schools have tennis teams. You can also

organize a match with friends.

Playing a few sets is an excellent way to practice and get some exercise. Do not forget to dress in loose, cool clothing. Shorts and T-shirts are popular choices.

It is a good idea to wear tennis shoes when you play. Most gym shoes will work. Just be certain that the rubber on the bottoms of your shoes is not too worn down. Also, be sure that the shoes are laced properly.

You will also need equipment and a place to play. You can buy tennis balls at most sports stores. They are usually sold in cans of three. A tennis

REAL WORLD MATH CHALLENGE

Gene needs to buy 3 cans of tennis balls for an upcoming match with his friends. The local athletic store is having a sale. Gene can get 1 set of 4 cans for $12.00. Each can contains 3 balls. **How many balls will he get with this deal?** Gene decides the sale is so good that he will buy an extra 2 sets of 4 cans. **What is the total number of balls Gene buys? How much does he spend?**

(Turn to page 29 for the answers)

Safe and reliable tennis equipment is more affordable now than ever.

ball is about the size of your fist. It is often covered with green, yellow,

orange, or white fabric.

You will need a racket, of course! The handle on a racket is covered

in leather or rubber. The racket's frame is lightweight and can be made

21st Century Content

Being a professional athlete can mean big bucks. Maria Sharapova became the first Russian female tennis player to be ranked number one when she was only 18 years old. In 2007, she was the world's highest-paid female athlete. She earned $23 million! Most of this money came from companies, such as Nike, that pay Sharapova to appear in advertisements for their products.

Athletes with huge earnings like these must learn to make responsible financial and economic choices. Why do you think companies turn to athletes like Sharapova to represent their products?

from different materials. These include graphite, aluminum, and fiberglass. Always choose a racket that does not feel too heavy or awkward in your hands.

Many public parks have tennis courts that you can use for practice. So do lots of fitness centers.

Do not worry if you are not an expert as soon as you pick up a racket. Always remember that tennis is supposed to be fun. You are sure to score if you use your math skills. You know addition, subtraction, multiplication, and division. Now it is time to test the strength of your serve!

REAL WORLD MATH CHALLENGE ANSWERS

Chapter One

Page 5

Jake has won 3 games so far.

5 games − 2 games = 3 games

C. J. has scored a total of 8 points.

2 games x 4 points = 8 points

Jake has scored a total of 12 points.

3 games x 4 points = 12 points

Chapter Two

Page 15

Bernard and Bella play a total of 10 games during the first set.

4 games + 6 games = 10 games

Bella wins 24 points.

6 games x 4 points = 24 points

Bernard wins 16 points.

4 games x 4 points = 16 points

Chapter Three

Page 19

Graf won 32 more singles matches than Agassi.

902 wins − 870 wins = 32 wins

She played as a pro for a total of 17 years.

1999 − 1982 = 17 years

This means she had an average of 53 wins each year.

902 wins ÷ 17 years = 53.05 = 53 wins

Agassi played as a pro for a total of 20 years.

2006 − 1986 = 20 years

This means he had an average of 44 wins each year.

870 wins ÷ 20 years = 43.5 = 44 wins

There is a difference of 9 wins between the players' career averages.

53 wins − 44 wins = 9 wins

Page 20

Agassi would have earned at least $84.6 million during the 3-year period between 2004 and 2006.

$28.2 million x 3 years = $84.6 million

Chapter Four

Page 22

Remember that Laver won twice. This means that men won 50 percent of the time.

3 men's wins ÷ 6 tournaments = 0.50 = 50%

Women also won 50 percent of the time.

3 women's wins ÷ 6 tournaments = 0.50 = 50%

A total of 3 players are from countries other than the United States.

5 players − 2 players = 3 players

Page 24

The total of Richards's and Navratilova's ages is 64 years.

15 years + 49 years = 64 years

The average of their ages is 32 years.

64 years ÷ 2 people = 32 years

A total of 88 years passed between the tournaments.

2006 − 1918 = 88 years

Chapter Five

Page 26

The sale allows Gene to get a total of 12 balls per set.

4 cans x 3 balls = 12 balls

He ends up buying 3 sets.

1 set + 2 sets = 3 sets

This means he purchases 36 balls.

3 sets x 12 balls = 36 balls

He spends $36.00.

$12.00 x 3 sets = $36.00

GLOSSARY

calendar year (KA-lehn-dur YEER) the period in a single year that runs from January 1 to December 31

opponent (uh-POH-nuhnt) a player on the other side or opposite team

professional (pruh-FESH-uh-nuhl) describing a sport that is played for money or as a career

statistics (steh-TISS-tiks) a branch of math that deals with the collection and interpretation of numbers and information

strokes (STROHKS) tennis moves that involve swinging at or hitting a ball with one's racket

titles (TYE-tuhlz) championships or wins

tournaments (TUR-nuh-muhnts) athletic competitions that involve a series of games to determine a winner

FOR MORE INFORMATION

Books

Donaldson, Madeline. *Venus & Serena Williams.*
Minneapolis: Lerner Publications, 2007.

Thomas, Ron, and Joe Herran. *Getting into Tennis.*
Philadelphia: Chelsea House Publishers, 2005.

Wells, Don. *For the Love of Tennis.* New York: Weigl Publishers, 2006.

Web Sites

International Tennis Hall of Fame
www.tennisfame.com
For information on tennis greats

United States Tennis Association
www.usta.com
Read players' profiles and learn tips on how to improve your game

Official Site of the U.S. Open
www.usopen.org
Information on the history of the U.S. Open

INDEX

ABOUT THE AUTHORS

Katie Marsico worked as a managing editor in children's publishing before becoming a freelance writer. She lives near Chicago, Illinois, with her husband and two children. She used to play tennis more often before her son and daughter were born. Ms. Marsico plans to make a comeback very soon, however, in order to beat her husband on the court.

Cecilia Minden, PhD, is a former classroom teacher and university professor. She now enjoys being a full-time author and consultant for children's books. She lives with her family near Chapel Hill, North Carolina. Dr. Minden's attempt at learning to play tennis gave her a better appreciation of the skill involved in being a good tennis player.